EARTH IN DANGER

WASTE & RECYCLING

By Emily Kington

Words that appear in **BOLD** are explained in the glossary.

First published by Hungry Tomato Ltd in 2022
F1, Old Bakery Studios, Blewetts wharf, Malpas Road, Truro, Cornwall, TR1 1QH, UK.

www.hungrytomato.com

ISBN 978-1-914087-62-2

A CIP catalog record for this book is available from the British Library.

Manufactured in the USA.

Picture credits (t=top, b=bottom, m=middle, l-left, r=right, bg=background)

Getty Images: 6-7bg, 25mr; 15br. IStock: 16tl. Jupiter Images: 26ml. Shutterstock: 10-11bg; 24br; 24Novembers 2bg; 7br; 4-5bg, 25t, 31bg; 89stocker 8bl; Air Images 16-17bg, 32b; Anna Hoychuk 12-13bg; blue-sea.cz 24m; Chaay_Tee 20-21bg, 30br; Fevziie 28ml; j.chizhe 22-23bg, 30tr; JARIRIYAWAT 1bg; Josep Curto 28b; KaliAntye 26br; M2020 18-19bg; Maples Images 10bl; Marina Lohrbach 3bg; New Africa 27br; Pwrmc 14-15bg; Rawpixel.com 8-9bg; RVillalon 29tr; Sheila Fitsgerald 27m; Sirtravelalot 18bl; Vera Larina 29b.

Every effort has been made to trace the copyright holders, and we apologize in advance for any unintentional omissions. We would be pleased to insert the appropriate acknowledgements in any subsequent edition of this publication.

CONTENTS

TOO MUCH TRASH!

Humans produce a lot of waste! We throw things away every day. While some of our garbage can be recycled or turned into compost, a lot of it ends up in the trash.

The trash we throw away can cause lots of problems for our planet.

Garbage can be harmful to wildlife and cause **pollution** in our water, soil and air.

Mostly, people and companies are becoming more aware of the problems with trash. Work is being done to reduce the amount of waste we all produce.

WHAT GETS DUMPED?

If we don't reuse or recycle things, they will end up on a **landfill** site like this one.

What kind of things end up in the trash? Should they really be there?

We throw out a lot of **organic waste.** This mostly comes from food waste, but can also include the remains of animals and plants. All of these things will rot away over time.

The rest of our trash is mostly made from plastic, glass, metal, or fabric (from old clothes).

Most of these things don't need to be thrown away. We can recycle or reuse them.

DID YOU KNOW?

A lot of food waste can be turned into compost. This can be added to soil to help grow plants.

Recycling is when you turn trash into something useful. This is important for many reasons.

Much of what we throw out is buried in holes in the ground, called landfills. If we keep making so much trash, there will be no space left to bury it!

There are limited amounts of **resources**, such as oil and metal. If we continue to take these out of the ground, one day they will completely run out. We need to find ways to recycle and reuse these materials.

DID YOU KNOW?

Plastic is made from oil, which is found underground. Supplies of oil are running out. It won't be long before there is none left.

WHY RECYCLE?

These days, almost everything can be recycled. Many things in your home may have been made from recycled items, such as newspapers, glass bottles and plastic containers.

Most of our paper and cardboard now gets recycled. Most of the corrugated cardboard used in **packaging** is recycled and has been used before.

Glass can be melted down and turned into new products again and again.

Many kinds of plastic can also be recycled, and used in many different products.

A machine for recycling metal cans.

RECYCLING EVERYDAY ITEMS

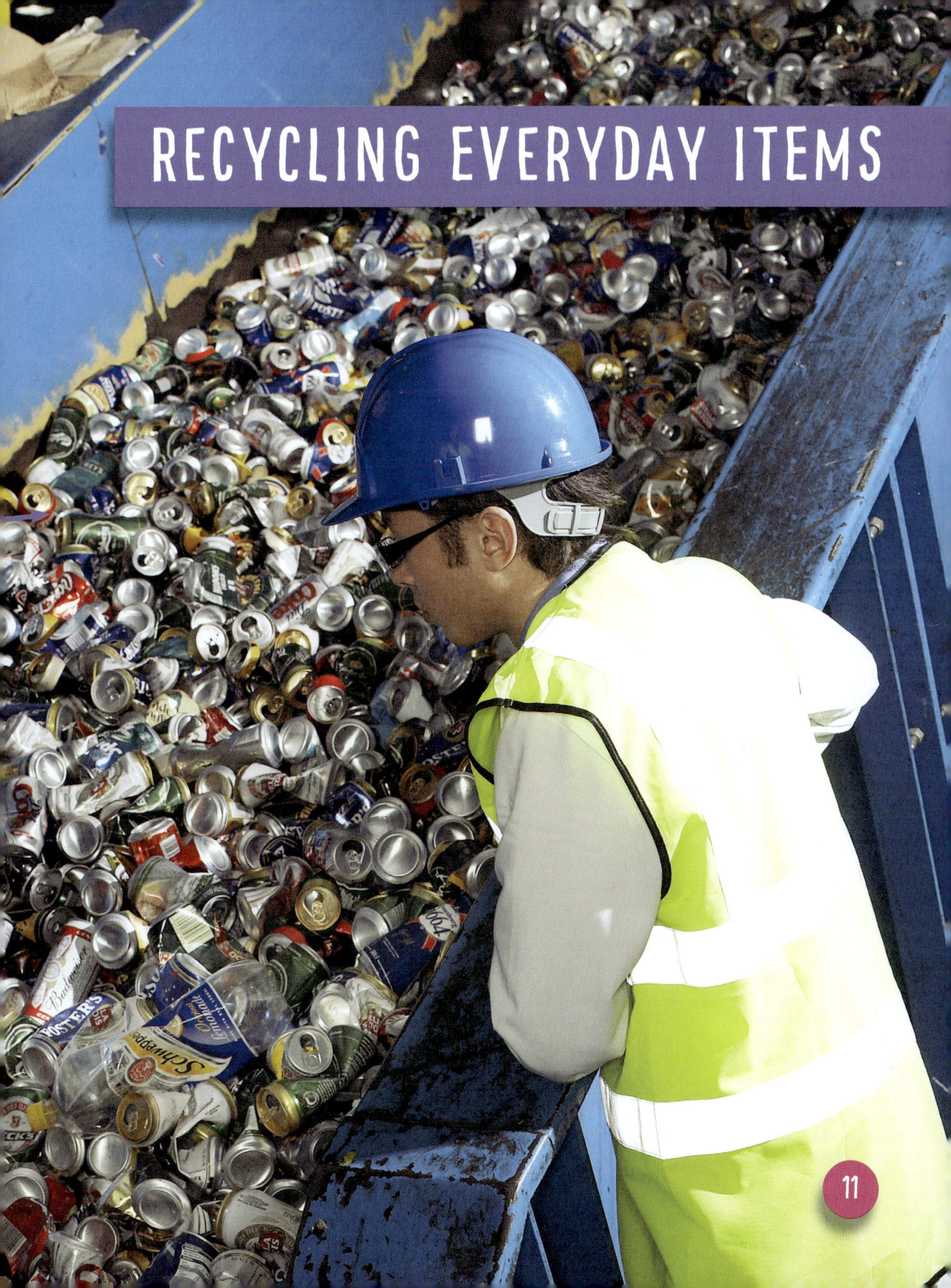

ORGANIC WASTE

Trash that will rot is called organic waste. Most of it is either old food or garden waste. This can be recycled too.

Lots of the food we buy ends up in the trash! Some of this is peelings from vegetables, and things we don't normally eat, such as bones from meat.

However, we could reduce food waste by saving leftovers and not buying more food than we need.

Some organic waste, such as vegetable peel, can be left to rot in special containers. After a while, the waste turns into compost. This can be added to soil to help plants grow more healthily.

DID YOU KNOW?

About one third of food that is produced around the world is wasted!

WHAT'S NOT RECYCLABLE?

Not all kinds of waste can be recycled. It is hard to recycle different materials when they are mixed together.

Some packaging, including lots of food wrappings, mixes plastic and metal. If the two different kinds of waste cannot be separated, they cannot be recycled.

Some chemical waste from factories is too dangerous and difficult to recycle. However, it doesn't need to end up in landfill. There are special facilities that can dispose of it safely.

People handling dangerous waste must wear special protective clothing.

MAKE IT BETTER!

In the past it was hard to recycle some kinds of waste. Technology has been moving fast and it is now possible to recycle many more types of trash.

Plastic was difficult to recycle because there are many different types. Now machines in **recycling plants** can separate most of them. This means that old plastic bottles can easily be turned into new ones, or other useful products!

Most large household items can now be recycled, and companies are working on ways to make their new products easier to recycle.

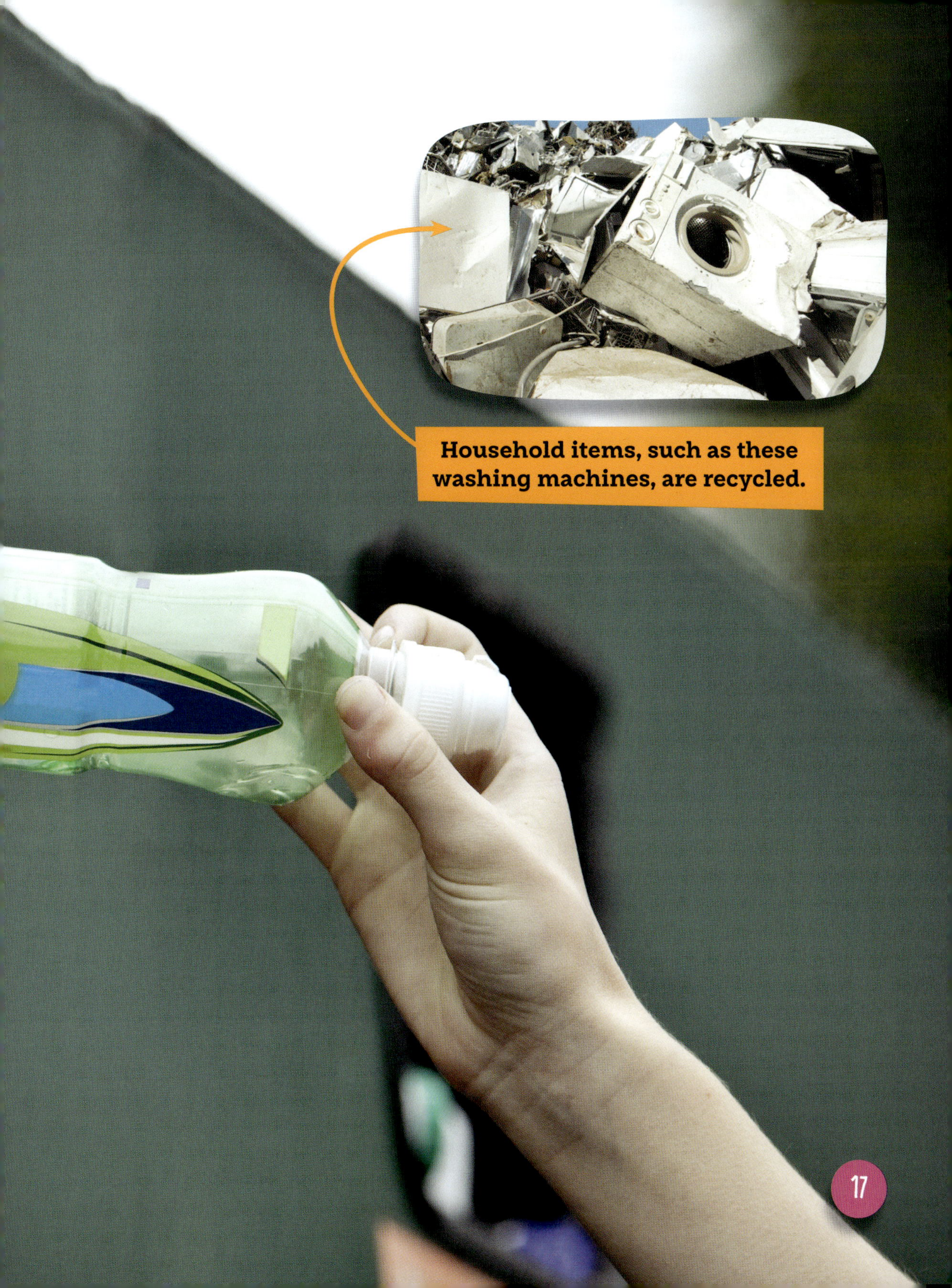

Household items, such as these washing machines, are recycled.

More and more towns and cities around the world have recycling centers. It is often possible to have your recycling picked up from outside your home.

Your recycling is then transported to facilities where it is sorted through into different types of **recyclables.**

Many towns and cities in different countries use slightly different methods for collecting recycling. It is important to read the guidelines for your local area to make sure you are recycling correctly.

DID YOU KNOW?

Don't try to recycle non-recyclable items. If they get mixed in with a batch of recycling, the whole lot may have to be sent to landfill!

Stacks of recycled paper in a truck at a recycling plant.

TRANSPORT & RECYCLING

Sometimes we throw things away that other people might find useful.

A huge amount of our old clothing and household items end up in landfill, even when they are still in useable condition.

Donating unwanted items to thrift stores is a great way to stop this from happening. What you think is trash might be treasure for somcone else!

Thrift stores are also great places to find new clothes, toys and other items for yourself. It is much cheaper than buying things new, and the money you do spend will often go to charity!

DID YOU KNOW?

Buying second hand items also saves resources, as less new items will have to be made.

TRASH OR TREASURE?

When it comes to trash, remember the three 'R's: Reduce, Reuse, Recycle.

Try to reduce how much trash you and your family produce. For example, take reusable shopping bags with you when you go to do any shopping.

Before you put anything in the trash, ask yourself if you could reuse it instead.

Make the effort to recycle and donate to thrift stores whenever possible.

Recycling still causes some pollution, and some of your items may not end up being recycled properly. However, it is still much better for the **environment** than sending things to landfills.

DID YOU KNOW?

Recycling one ton of paper saves 7,000 gallons of water.

HOW TO MAKE A DIFFERENCE

FACT FILE

LANDFILL

Here are some of the major problems with landfills:

Trash is polluting the ocean and coral reefs.

- Harmful chemicals can leak out of waste in landfills and seep into the ground. This can poison the soil and water supply, making people and wildlife that live nearby ill.

- We are running out of places for landfills.
- Landfills are often full of materials that could have been recycled.

DID YOU KNOW?

Lots of our trash ends up in the ocean. This causes pollution and is very harmful to ocean wildlife.

- Food waste that ends up in landfill produces large amounts of a gas called **methane**. Too much methane can increase **global warming**.

FACT FILE

MAKE YOUR OWN COMPOST

It's easy to make compost from your food and garden waste. Compost is great for your yard or garden, as it makes soil healthier and helps plants grow well.

You can buy a compost bin, or make your own out of recycled wood, like this one.

What to put in your compost bin:

- Peelings from fruits and vegetables.
- Egg shells and unbleached teabags can be added, but they can take a long time to break down.
- Weeds, prunings and grass cuttings.
- Crumpled waste paper and cardboard, but not too much.

What not to put in your compost bin:

- Meat scraps, or any cooked food.
- Thick branches or roots.
- Anything that has been sprayed with chemicals.

- It's a good idea to stir the mixture each time you add new waste.
- It can take six to nine months for your compost to be ready to use.
- It should look like dark brown soil, and be cool to the touch.

FACT FILE

RE-USE & RECYCLE

In the past, glass bottles were reused. They were collected, cleaned, and filled again.

Now most glass bottles are used only once and then recycled. Then they can be melted and turned into new bottles.

What are the advantages of reusing?

- It saves on the energy needed to make new ones. This means less pollution.
- We don't have to use fresh materials to make them.

So, why don't we do this?

- Collecting, sorting, transporting and cleaning bottles uses a lot of energy.
- Bottles are easily damaged and can only be used a few times.
- Bottles for reuse have to be stronger than bottles used only once, and so they use more materials.

Whether we decide to recycle or reuse, we should never simply throw glass away!

Bottles being made in a factory.

HOW YOU CAN HELP

TAKE ACTION!

- Donate unwanted clothes, toys and home goods to thrift stores.
- Instead of buying presents or greetings cards, try making them from recycled materials.
- Carry reusable shopping bags and a refillable water bottle to save on waste when you're out of the house.

SCHOOL PROJECT

Find out about all the materials that can be recycled and make a display at your school. This will help other people learn about recycling.

GLOSSARY

compost Natural material that has rotted and can be added to the soil to improve it.

environment The surroundings or conditions in which a person, animal, or plant lives or operates.

global warming The warming of the planet's air and oceans as a result of a build-up of greenhouse gases in the atmosphere.

landfill Big holes in the ground that are filled with trash and waste.

methane A gas given off when material rots. It can be burned to give heat to make electricity.

organic waste Material that once was living, including food, plants, animal remains, or human and animal waste.

packaging Glass, plastic, paper and metal materials used to wrap goods that are for sale.

pollution Unwanted chemicals and other substances that harm the air, water, or land.

recyclables Objects made out of material that can be recycled and reused.

recycle To turn unwanted materials into something useful.

recycling plants Factories where recycling goes to be sorted.

resources Everything we need for life, such as water, food, fuel and energy.

INDEX